Helping children become better readers

For parents, caregivers, teachers and aides

Patricia Hipwell

Dedication

To my dear friend, Kim, who spent a lifetime enhancing children's literacy development. This book is for you.

First Edition published 2021

A catalogue record for this book is available from the National Library of Australia

ISBN: 9780987215956 (paperback)

Typeset in Roboto 10pt.

Text and cover design: Watson Ferguson & Company
Editing and proofreading: Charlotte Cottier AE

Cover image by wavebreakmedia/Shutterstock.com
Inside illustration by Zdenek Sasek/Shutterstock.com

Self published by logonliteracy

Printed in China by Everbest Printing Investment Limited.

Contents

Introduction

While not everyone agrees that reading is one of life's pleasures, few would dispute that reading is an essential skill for a rich and full life. Most children learn to read and read well. However, too many children struggle and become adept at avoiding reading because they find it difficult. To become better at anything, we have to do more of it; therefore, it is critical to support struggling readers to persist with reading.

Many caregivers enjoy helping children learn to read. But some find this experience a source of anxiety and frustration, leading to negative attitudes to reading, which can be destructive. One reason learning to read can be a tense time for caregivers and children is that help is not always helpful. Unless you have learnt how to teach children to read, it is unlikely you will know how to do it. You may have a vague memory of how you learnt or what your teachers and caregivers said to you. Despite your best efforts, though, some of what you do as you support your child has the potential to *turn them off* reading. Home reading, far from being a pleasurable experience, can be a time of tears, anxiety and frustration, and that's not just for the child!

This book allows you to identify the reading behaviours (some good, some poor) of your child and take appropriate action. It aims to make sure that as you support your child you do so using what research shows are the best ways to assist.

There is a strong correlation between vocabulary development and reading, and the book provides more information about this. We know that children who know more words are better readers. They read more, and more easily, because they know more words and, therefore, learn more words. You can do a great deal to develop your child's vocabulary through oral (spoken) language. The book includes suggestions and tips about ways to promote vocabulary development.

Spelling is important too, so the book also includes some ideas for assisting children to become better spellers.

Patricia Hipwell

2021

Key terms

The definitions provided here are those relating to an educational/reading context only; some terms may have other meanings in different contexts.

aliteracy	A form of literacy where readers choose not to read conventional text such as books but may engage with a large amount of text through their use of electronic media.
audience	The person or people for whom the text has been written. Language choices in texts are determined by the audience.
author's purpose	The reason/s the author has written the text. Purposes include to entertain, inform, persuade, instruct, reflect.
automaticity	The ability to recognise words quickly and precisely.
close reading	Looking at a piece of text in a focused way. Readers may 'linger longer' over the text, paying close attention to the key parts.
cognitive load	The amount of 'work' demanded of the brain at one time. The cognitive load of reading is very high.
comprehension	Making sense of text.
contextual clues	Evidence in the text to assist with making meaning, especially inferring.
continuous reading	The practice of reading (usually prose) without stopping. This is the way most readers read novels.
decoding	The ability to say (pronounce) written words. It relies on knowledge of letters and sounds and the many sounds letters make individually and when combined. Rapid, accurate and efficient decoding frees up working memory to concentrate on meaning.
dialogue	A conversation between two or more people that can be written or spoken.
direct speech	The words actually spoken by characters in stories or narrative non-fiction. For example: *'I'm tired,' complained Polly. 'Can I go home?'* Speech marks or quotation marks assist the reader with identifying direct speech.
environmental print	The printed texts that are part of everyday life; includes signs, billboards, labels, and business logos.
etymology	The study of the origin and historical development of a particular word's form and meaning.
fiction	Stories that are not true.
finger pointing	The practice of pointing to a word before reading it. Readers who finger point tend to read individual words in a stilted way (sometimes referred to as 'barking at print') rather than fluently and expressively.

Key terms

fluency	The ability to read quickly, naturally, smoothly, with expression and few errors. Fluent readers recognise words automatically and group words together (phrasing) quickly.
high-frequency words	The words that occur most often in written material (e.g. *and, the, to, when, if*). They are grammatical words (determiners, prepositions, conjunctions, pronouns, auxiliary verbs) that usually don't have much meaning on their own but contribute greatly to the meaning of a sentence. They are the 'glue' words that hold the 'content' words (nouns, verbs, adjectives and adverbs) together to make sentences. Some of them can be sounded out using basic phonics rules (e.g. *had, it, by*), but many of them are not phonically regular (see 'sight words' below). They often have an abstract, grammatical meaning that's difficult to explain to a child.
home readers	The books children bring home from school to practise reading. Home readers should be familiar to children and easy enough to read so that children can practise reading and thereby become more confident, fluent and able to read with expression.
indirect speech	The essence of what was said but may not be word for word; often called reported speech. For example: *Polly complained that she was tired and asked if she could go home.* We do not know the exact words Polly said, only the essence of what she said. Quotation marks are not used for indirect speech.
inference	The practice of gaining meaning from text by making an interpretation beyond the literal information given in the text. Readers' responses are based on information in the text and can be backed up by what is there. Inference does not involve wild guessing. Different readers make different inferences depending on their experience and prior knowledge.
keywords	The words in a text that relate to its main topic.
levelled readers	Books that are at different levels of difficulty from very easy to more complex and challenging. Most reading schemes level their books. Teachers give students books at an appropriate level of difficulty to match with where the students are currently reading. This ensures they gain confidence as readers.
literal meaning	What is directly stated in the text. The reader does not have to search for the meaning; it is 'right there'.
modelling	A common practice in education that involves the teacher or caregiver demonstrating the behaviour they want to see in the child. For example, if you want your child to become a more fluent reader, then model fluency and show how it is done.
non-fiction	Texts that are factual or true.

Key terms

one-to-one correspondence	The concept of one word spoken being equivalent to one word written. In other words, the child reads the exact number of words on the page, neither too many nor too few.
onset	The initial or beginning sound of a word.
phoneme	The smallest unit of sound in a word that makes one word different from another.
phonemic awareness	The ability to hear individual sounds in words. It is generally agreed that the 26 letters of the alphabet make 44 sounds.
phonological awareness	Sensitivity to sounds in speech; for example, rhyming words or words beginning with the same sound, such as *shout, shove, shine*.
phrasing	The practice of reading words in groups rather than word by word; helps children become fluent readers.
point of error	The place in the reading where a mistake occurs.
predicting	The practice of guessing what a text might be about or what could happen in a text based on what is seen or has been read so far.
prior knowledge	What we already know about a topic.
punctuation	Standard symbols such as full stops, commas, question marks and so on inserted in writing or printing to organise it into phrases and sentences and to make the meaning clear.
reading prompts	A variety of phrases spoken by the listener to encourage the reader to either have a go or self-correct; for example: *Get your mouth ready for the beginning sound. You said … Does that look right/sound right/make sense?*
reading strategy	A skill or technique readers use to help them make sense of text. Strategies include predicting, monitoring and self-correcting, phrasing and rereading.
rereading	The practice of reading a text more than once. This helps with both comprehension and enjoyment.
retelling	A common practice used to assess if the reader has any memory of what they have read. After reading, they will often be asked: *Tell me what the story is about.*
rime	The remaining sound that follows the onset (beginning sound) of a word.
scanning	The practice of looking for specific information; may involve finding information to answer questions.
self-correction	The ability of a reader to recognise they have made a mistake and to correct it when reading; may involve having another go at the word, going back to the start of the sentence or saying, 'That didn't make sense.' Possibly the most important of all reading behaviours.

Key terms

self-monitoring	The practice of readers listening to their reading and realising when they have made a mistake or meaning breaks down (doesn't sound right, look right or make sense).
sight words	High-frequency words that are difficult to sound out because they are phonically irregular (e.g. *said, was, of*); therefore, they need to be learnt by sight rather than sound.
silent reading	The practice of readers reading the words in their heads, not aloud.
skimming	The practice of browsing or glancing over a text. Readers are not necessarily looking for anything specific; rather, they are gaining an idea of what the text is about.
sounding out	The practice of saying each sound in a word slowly and then blending the sounds together and saying them more quickly; for example, *h-o-t* (individual sounds) and then *hot* (blended sounds).
summarising	The practice of reducing a text to a few key ideas; details are omitted.
sweet spot	The point in a story where the reader becomes hooked and wants to find out what is going to happen next.
syllable	A unit of pronunciation with one vowel sound with or without surrounding consonants that forms the whole or part of a word. For example, the word *story* has two syllables: *stor/y*. It is usual to break up the syllables with a solidus (/).
syntax	The way words are arranged to form grammatically correct phrases and sentences in a language.
text	The wording of anything written or printed; may include stories, information texts, poems, explanations, and so on.
text comprehension	The ability of the reader to understand what they are reading or hearing.
tracking	The ability of the reader to move their eyes smoothly across text.
visualising	The practice of the reader or listener forming pictures in their mind based on what they are reading or hearing. It's a good idea to do this at different points of the reading (i.e. before, during and after reading).
vocabulary knowledge	The reader having a bank of words they recognise *on sight* as well as knowledge about words, their meanings and pronunciations.
word recognition	The ability to literally see a word and know it. The more words readers can recognise without having to think about them the better readers they become.

What is reading?

Reading is a problem-solving activity where readers make meaning from, and sense of, what they have read. Just being able to 'say' words is not reading. It is decoding, and children who can decode, often quite well, may be making no meaning at all from their reading.

To make meaning, readers use information from two sources. First, they draw on knowledge and experience in their minds. Second, they draw on the information present in the text. The narrower the gap between the two sources, the more likely it is that meaning is constructed. One of the problems children face as they move through their schooling is that they do not have adequate knowledge of important words or concepts in the subjects they study. If children are unable to comprehend written text, they are unlikely to be able to demonstrate their knowledge through writing.

Because reading is a problem-solving activity, making mistakes is a key part of learning to read. We need to encourage children to feel comfortable about the mistakes they make. If they are discouraged by them, they are likely to struggle with reading and ultimately avoid it.

What do readers need?

Readers need to be able to translate or decode the marks on the page or screen. When referring to the written word, the marks are letters and punctuation. Letters have sounds, both singularly and in combination with other letters, and combine to make words. Several words together form phrases and sentences. A collection of sentences forms a paragraph, and paragraphs combine to make longer stretches of text such as found in essays or books.

To read text, readers need to:

- recognise words easily and quickly
- focus on the meaning of words
- understand the meaning of most words they encounter
- apply knowledge about words and language to work out how to say unknown words and decipher their possible meanings
- make sense of what they read.

Good readers need:

1. **Phonological awareness**. They can hear words and know that words are made up of smaller units of sound called *phonemes*. If children can break up words into the sound segments of those words, then they have one of the skills necessary for good reading.
2. **A knowledge of the alphabetical principle**. They know the letters and the sounds those letters make. This is phonics. Because there are 26 letters in the alphabet and 44 sounds, they are aware that some letters can make more than one sound, especially the vowels. For example, think of the different sound that *a* makes in the following words: *another*, *chance*, *accept*, *cake* and *water*.
3. **Fluency**. They read smoothly and naturally, in the way of speaking. Being able to decode written words into spoken words quickly, automatically and efficiently (automaticity) is essential for fluent reading.
4. **Vocabulary knowledge**. The more words children know and the more words they have heard before they encounter them in their reading, the better readers they are likely to be. Exposure to words comes through children's books and spoken language. Having heard a word before encountering it in print is especially helpful.

What do readers need?

5. **Comprehension**. It sounds obvious but understanding what we read is the most important aspect of reading. What is the point of just being able to say the words? Comprehension is improved where children have a well-developed and good general knowledge.

Children who start school with phonological awareness and good general language skills are far more likely to read easily and quickly.

Reading *to*, *with* and *by* children

Reading can be part of the home environment in several ways. Reading *to* children involves a reader (usually a better one) reading aloud. Reading *with* children shares the reading between reader and listener. Reading *by* children is where the child does all the reading.

Choose the type of reading depending on the time of day, the mood of the reader and caregiver and the purpose of reading. If your child is a reluctant reader, encourage them to read to you most of the time, that is, reading *by* children. It is fine, however, to read *with* them and *to* them as well. It is a good idea to ask them which one they would like to do. Reluctant readers gain confidence by selecting the approach. Be careful, though, that they do not always choose the option that allows them to avoid reading. Frustration is the enemy of learning, so always ensure children do not become frustrated when reading. If you sense this is happening, take over until their mood improves.

Reading *to*

Children of any age enjoy being read to. Do not stop reading to your child just because they can read. Reading to children is a good opportunity for you to share your love of reading and what reading means to you. It can be a wise strategy when you or your child are tired and you can see that getting them to read to you is going to be a struggle. Reading to children is also an ideal chance to model fluency, expression, working out what words mean and predicting.

Reading *with*

Reading with children is an opportunity to expose children to books that may be too difficult for them to read independently. With a book that is easier and more familiar, you might take turns at reading. Sometimes you can read *over the top of* them and carry them through more difficult words or sections. Young children enjoy reading some parts of the story (often a repeated line). Reading with children and asking them to follow with their eyes is a way of reading more difficult text or text that is about an unfamiliar topic. Reading with children provides a valuable opportunity to talk about books, the vocabulary in books, the intention of the author, messages in the book and more.

Reading *by*

Children learning to read need to read all types of texts. At school, the teacher has a limited amount of time during which they can listen to your child. Therefore, it is important that caregivers and other family members listen to children on a regular basis. Reading by children aloud is a way that caregivers and teachers can monitor the child's progress and where and with what they need help. Reading aloud is the main way listeners can know what is going on in a child's head during the process of reading; therefore, it is something we ask children to do a great deal in the early years of schooling. As children become more experienced readers and caregivers are confident that their children can read, reading *by* is often done silently without a listener.

Children's reading behaviours

Reading behaviours of successful and independent readers

BEFORE READING

- understand that reading is a sense-making process
- read at or above grade level
- build up their background knowledge on the subject before they begin to read
- know their purpose for reading
- approach reading with interest and enthusiasm
- know there are a variety of fiction and non-fiction texts
- enjoy a variety of books and other reading material
- do not avoid reading
- read for pleasure
- may be able to articulate who their favourite authors are and why
- enjoy being read to
- show an interest in the meaning of words and know the meaning of many words
- recognise contextual clues
- have etymological knowledge of words (roots, affixes [prefixes and suffixes])
- consciously draw on prior knowledge to make meaning

DURING READING

- are confident and optimistic that reading will make sense
- realise when they have made a mistake and self-correct it
- give their complete attention to the reading task
- adjust their reading rate to match the purpose for reading and the type of reading material
- monitor their reading comprehension aand do it so often that it becomes automatic
- draw on a range of strategies when trying to understand the author's message and match them to reading materials
- stop reading only to use a fix-up strategy when they do not understand
- use punctuation to assist with making meaning
- persist with reading
- use the position of the word in the sentence to help work out meaning
- may not read every word but know when attention to detail is important
- read fluently and with expression by varying volume, pitch and pace
- look ahead to the next group of words, especially if they are reading aloud
- are not discouraged when they make errors because they know this is part of the reading process
- pay attention to language signals that link to the content and give meaning. These are usually the non-content words on which teaching rarely focuses (e.g. *due to, generally, whereas, finally*)
- make links between parts of the text to assist with meaning (e.g. between a picture and words)
- notice the beginnings and ends of words, especially plurals

AFTER READING

- can talk about books and relate what they read to their own lives
- try to use the new words they encounter
- like to talk about their reading
- choose reading as a pastime
- can evaluate whether they have achieved their purpose for reading
- respond critically and personally to what they have read
- can evaluate their own comprehension of what was read
- search for books by the same author of a book they have enjoyed
- seek additional information from other sources
- carry reading material with them
- request books as presents
- belong to a library
- can summarise the main ideas of a text
- can retell a story
- will reread books they have enjoyed
- like to share parts of the reading by reading aloud something of interest to themselves and possibly others
- have fond memories of books they have enjoyed
- will read to younger siblings
- enjoy listening when others are talking about reading
- resist the lure of technology in favour of a good book

Reading behaviours of less successful and struggling readers

BEFORE READING

- think that reading is just about saying the words (decoding)
- read below grade level
- may complain about the length of the text they are required to read
- do not expect reading to make sense and are not surprised when it doesn't
- have little or no background knowledge about the topic so have nothing to which new knowledge might 'stick'
- start reading without thinking about the topic, structure or language of the text
- are unsure of their purpose for reading and do not realise there are many different purposes for reading
- approach reading with very little interest or enthusiasm
- are unlikely to know the difference between fiction and non-fiction texts
- avoid reading whenever they can and convey negative attitudes to reading (e.g. 'This is boring! I hate reading!')
- do not see reading as pleasurable and, as a result, resist any encouragement to read
- are likely to enjoy being read to more than they enjoy reading for themselves
- have a limited vocabulary
- rely heavily on 'sounding out' as the strategy for working out unknown words
- have limited etymological knowledge of words (roots, affixes [prefixes and suffixes])

DURING READING

- do not expect reading to make sense, so their self-correction strategies are weak
- lack reading stamina
- are easily distracted from the reading task – will happily talk rather than read
- are easily defeated by the reading process – will become angry and frustrated when they stumble, make errors or can't read some of the words
- tend to read at the same rate (usually slowly and in a laboured way) and lack the skills to adjust their reading rate to match the purpose for reading and the type of reading material
- do not monitor their reading comprehension – often cannot say whether they understand or they don't
- have few strategies on which to draw and tend to read every text using one or two strategies
- have no other ways to gain meaning when something does not work
- keep reading even though it is clear they do not understand what they have read
- do not monitor their own reading, so often fail to realise they have made a mistake; mistakes have to be pointed out to them
- do not use punctuation to help make meaning – will often ignore full stops
- read one word at a time, rather than in phrases, with limited expression
- put so much energy into decoding that they are unable to vary volume, pitch and pace of reading to enhance meaning
- do not look ahead but focus on one word at a time, making fluency difficult
- are likely to encounter problems with more than 1 in 10 words

AFTER READING

- do not talk about books and what they have read as part of their general conversation
- may show some interest in words and enjoy hearing new words, especially in less formal situations than school
- are unlikely to try to use new words that they encounter
- avoid reading as a pastime
- are not sure of why they have read a text; therefore, are unable to evaluate whether they have achieved the purpose for reading
- show little interest in responding to what they have read
- cannot articulate whether understanding has occurred
- are unlikely to have read many books
- are happy to read as required by various forms of technology they use
- do not request books as presents
- often focus on details rather than main ideas
- struggle to remember all the events in a story
- see reading of a text as something that is done once
- are unlikely to want to share anything that they have read
- do not find reading pleasurable, so memories of reading tend to evoke negative emotions
- may find that their siblings are better readers and be embarrassed by this, especially when the sibling is younger
- will probably find something else to do when others are talking about reading
- cannot resist the lure of technology over reading a book

BEFORE READING	DURING READING	AFTER READING
	• ignore language signals that link to the content and give meaning. These are usually the non-content words on which teaching rarely focuses (e.g. *due to, generally, whereas, finally*) • fail to realise that some words are more significant than others in making meaning • have difficulty making links between parts of the text, often because they are so focused on one part of it • ignore the beginnings and ends of words, especially plurals • do not use the position of the word in the sentence to help them work out meaning • are unable to distinguish between when it is important to read every word and when it isn't • are likely to struggle with home reading, leading to stress for their caregivers	

Reading behaviours expected in a child who is making appropriate progress by age eight

Source: Annandale K, Bindon R, Handley K, Johnston A, Lockett L & Lynch P (2004b). *STEPS professional development: First Steps, reading map of development*, 2nd edn, Rigby Heinemann, Port Melbourne, Victoria.

Early readers recognise a bank of frequently used words and use a small range of strategies to comprehend texts. These include short literary texts and structured informational texts that have familiar vocabulary and are supported by illustrations. Reading of unfamiliar texts is often slow and deliberate as they focus on exactly what is on the page, using sounding out as a primary word-identification strategy.

Use of texts

- Reads and demonstrates comprehension of texts by:
    - recalling key information explicit in a text
    - identifying the main idea explicit in a text
    - selecting events to retell a text, sometimes including unnecessary events or information
    - linking explicit ideas in a text, e.g. comparing a character at different points in the text.
- Locates and selects text appropriate to purpose, interest and readability, e.g. uses library systems, skims contents page.

Children's reading behaviours

Contextual understanding

- Expresses and justifies personal responses to texts, e.g. 'I didn't like ... because ... '.
- Understands that authors and illustrators select information to suit a purpose and an audience.
- Recognises how characters, people and events are represented, and offers suggestions for alternatives.

Conventions

- Recognises a bank of frequently used words in different contexts, e.g. high-frequency words, personally significant words.
- Recognises all letters by name and their regular sound.
- Explains how known text forms vary by stating:
    - purpose, e.g. *procedures instruct*
    - some elements of organisation, e.g. *procedures have headings*
    - some elements of structure, e.g. *procedures list materials and steps.*

Processes and strategies

- Draws upon a small knowledge base to comprehend, e.g. sight vocabulary, concept and text-structure knowledge
- Uses a small range of strategies to comprehend, e.g. self-questioning, adjusting reading rate
- Determines unknown words by using word-identification strategies, e.g. decoding using phonemes, onset and rime
- Focuses on decoding words accurately when reading an unfamiliar text, which may result in limited fluency, expression and loss of meaning.

Should I be concerned about my child's progress?

In all areas of physical, emotional, social, psychological and educational development, children develop at different rates. With reading, it is sometimes difficult to say where children should be at a given age. However, many tests are available to give an idea of a child's reading age compared with their chronological age. If a caregiver suspects a child is not where they should be, it is important to act quickly and early. An initial gap becomes a large one very quickly and can make reading a lifelong struggle. So, don't delay – early intervention makes the most difference.

One or more of the following behaviours in a child who is learning to read may indicate cause for concern:

- cannot say all the letters of the alphabet and does not know the sounds these letters make
- cannot identify different sounds made by the same letter in different words (e.g. *a* in *ant, banana, zebra, swan, ball*)
- cannot identify rhyming words
- cannot identify the beginning, middle and end sounds of words when you say the words
- is unable to clap or count syllables
- speaks poorly and is difficult to understand, especially by school age
- talks very little
- shows little interest in books and does not interact with them
- does not ask questions or cannot answer questions you ask when you read to them
- does not relate the book to their own lives
- appears helpless and hopeless and becomes easily discouraged
- makes comments such as 'I hate reading. Reading is boring.'
- does not know that there are clues in the text to help work out words or cannot use those clues.

If you are concerned about your child's progress, talk to their teacher and the principal of their school as soon as possible. Do not delay – remember that, without intervention, a small gap quickly becomes a large one.

Guidelines for caregivers

Reading a book for the first time

If your child has selected or brings home a book they have not read before, there are several things you can do to make the reading successful. Before reading commences, try some of the following:

- If necessary (e.g. with very young children), talk about how to hold the book, how to turn the pages, where to begin reading and where to restart reading after finishing a line.
- Ensure the child can identify the following components of the book: title, author, illustrator, blurb, illustrations, written text.
- Read the title to the child and ask them to repeat it. Explain the difference between non-fiction and fiction books and ask them to tell you the type of book they think it is. They can give reasons for their prediction.
- Ask them to predict what the book is about. Do not evaluate the prediction. Say: *When you read the book, you'll be able to see how close you were with your prediction.*
- 'Walk' through the book, pointing out what is happening. Be careful not to give too much away as this takes away the need to read. You can ask questions such as:
  - *What do you think is happening here?*
  - *What might this character be saying?*
  - *Why do you think there's a picture of ... ?*
- During and after the reading, you can demonstrate curiosity by saying, for example:
  - *I wonder why the character is ...*
  - *I wonder what will happen next; I think that ... will say/do ...*
  - *I wasn't really expecting that to happen.*
  - *This reminds me of another book we read about ...*
- Pre-teach any vocabulary you think will be challenging (see page 75).
- Identify some of the punctuation, especially that which indicates direct speech.
- Give a purpose for reading, for example: *When you've finished reading the book, I am going to get you to tell me what happened / tell me what you think the message is / identify the main idea.*

The role of the listener

A listener's intervention may be premature and destructive to a reader's search for meaning and accuracy. Therefore, it is important that the listener knows how to listen and respond.

- Make time to listen to the child read every day in a place where there are no distractions from technology.
- Give your close attention and show interest in the story.
- Be patient and do not rush the reading even though you may have other things to do.
- Ask: *Do you think these words might be in the book?* (Say a few words to which the child responds whether they think those words will be in the book. You can ask them why.)
- Intervene in such a way that the child makes their own decisions about the meaning of words/phrase and sentences.
- Telling is sometimes necessary but make it a last resort.
- Encourage the child to say if the book is too difficult for them.
- Ignore minor errors that do not affect meaning.
- Draw attention to words and talk about the meaning of new or unfamiliar words. Try to use these words in conversation.
- Develop some prompts to use when a child encounters a word they don't know. For example, you might say:
    - *It means ...*
    - *Leave it for a moment and read on.*
    - *See if you can come back to the word after reading the sentence again.*
- Give some wait time and avoid prompting too early. Good readers solve their own problems and need time to do this.

Guidelines for caregivers

The four Ps for listeners

Pause: Be patient while the child is trying to work out the text. Curb your natural instinct to come to their assistance.

Prompt: If the child is distressed when they don't know a word, remind them of the strategies they can use. For example, they can read on to the end of the sentence, start again and read the whole sentence, or look at the first letter for a clue. Tell them the word after they have made two attempts. (See Appendix A for more prompts.)

Praise: Be enthusiastic about all attempts to make sense. Sometimes what they read is different from the printed text. This is acceptable if the basic meaning is not changed. Whenever children self-correct to regain meaning, praise them. For example, you might say: *Good, now it makes sense.* (See Appendix B for more examples of comments for praising a child's reading behaviours.)

Probe: When children lose meaning, ask them a question that will help them to focus on meaning. For example, *Does that make sense?* rather than, *That doesn't make sense.* This puts the onus on the reader to monitor their own reading, which is what good readers do.

Responding to children's reading behaviours

How this section of the book is organised

This section of the book is organised in the following way:

If your child ...	This identifies the reading behaviour.
Then:	This provides a possible reason or reasons for the behaviour.
So, you can:	These are suggested ways to respond to the behaviour. Choose from several suggestions.
This is because:	These are the reasons for the suggested ways to respond.
In a nutshell:	This is a summary of the main points.

If your child appears to be reading the book from memory

(e.g. They may retell the story with words that are different from the printed words.)

Then:

They see reading as something that must be done for the teacher, the parent or school generally. They may think that this is the ultimate aim of reading.

So, you can:

- Ask them to point to the words as they read (but see 'If your child points to the words with their finger as they read' on page 54).
- Ask them to point to particular words.
- Repeat what they said and ask them if there were enough words or too many words on the page.

This is because:

- Memorising words is not a bad thing to do. Good readers have many words in their long-term memories.
- Ultimately readers must learn that reading is about reading the words not just making up a commentary to go with the story.
- One-to-one correspondence is an essential reading behaviour.
- The right messages about reading include that reading must make sense and that the same number of words should be read as are on the page.

In a nutshell:

- Children should know that they should read as many words as there are on the page – no more, no fewer.
- Good readers pay attention to and read every word.
- We need to give the right messages about reading, not the wrong ones.

If your child becomes frustrated when you say *sound it out*

Then:

This strategy may not be particularly helpful and they will need other strategies to try.

So, you can:

- Use prompts other than *sound it out.*
- Say: *Look at the picture for a clue. Are there any letters and sounds in the word that are familiar to you? What word would make sense here? Look at the beginning letters, do you know what sound they make? Get your mouth ready for the word.*
- Before frustration kicks in, tell them the word. Say: *I am going to tell you the word, then I want you to tell me how I know it is that word.* (There might be some familiar letter clusters or something in the picture that helps.)
- At the end of the reading, go back to the sentence with the tricky word and ask the child to reread it a couple of times. Ask: *Where was the tricky word? What are you going to do to help remember it for next time?*

This is because:

- Good readers have a variety of strategies to try when they come across an unknown word.
- Sounding out can help if the reader has heard the word before but is not helpful if they haven't.
- Frustration is the enemy of learning; we need to do all we can to avoid the reader becoming frustrated.
- Telling is a last resort; we want to give readers the tools to work out words for themselves.

In a nutshell:

- Always wait – be patient.
- Always prompt with prompts other than *sound it out.*
- Tell as a last resort.
- Encourage the reader to think of a way they will remember the word.

If your child can answer questions where the answers are 'right there' (literal) but not questions where the answers are 'hidden' (inferential)

Then:

They can make meaning from the text at a literal ('right there') level but do not realise that often they need to 'think and search' for the meaning (inference).

So, you can:

- Talk about where the answer lies. Say: *Is the answer 'right there'? Do you have to 'think and search'? Or are you 'on your own'?*
- Give readers some background knowledge of the topic of the book. For example, if the book is about crocodiles, then ask what the child knows about them. If they know nothing or very little, fill in the gaps and tell them about the topic so they have the background knowledge to make an inference.
- Say: *This is a tricky question to answer because it doesn't actually say so in the text; we have to think about what we know.*
- Ask questions that require the child to think more deeply about the text (see Appendix E for ideas and question prompts to help children develop inferential skills).
- Use real-world examples. For example: *Mum picks up the phone and starts smiling and laughing. What can we infer? She has received some good news; she's happy to be speaking to the person on the phone; someone has told her a joke or funny story.* These are all reasonable inferences. Unreasonable inferences might include: *It's bad news; she dislikes the person; it is a telemarketer.*

This is because:

- To infer requires information from the text and background knowledge.
- If your child does not have background knowledge of the topic, then making an inference is difficult.
- Providing the background knowledge assists with making an inference.
- Your child will not learn how to make an inference if questions are always literal.

In a nutshell:

- Not all answers to questions can be easily found in the text.
- Talk about where the answer to a question lies. Is it 'right there', 'think and search' or 'on your own'?
- Build background knowledge of the topic as this helps with making an inference.
- Give the child some real-world examples.
- Ask inferential questions.

If your child cannot hear the vowel sounds in words or distinguish between the vowel and the consonant sounds

Then:

They have not yet learnt the sounds that letters make and the difference between vowel and consonant sounds.

So, you can:

- Ask your child which letters make a particular sound.
- Compare the sounds that the same letters make in different words.
- Explain to your child that all vowels have at least two pronunciations: a short and a long sound. For example, in the word *say*, the ***a*** sounds like ***ay*** and so is a long vowel sound. Compare this with the word *cat* where the vowel sound is a short ***a***.
- As you drive around, look at environmental print and comment on which letters make sounds in words. For example, say: *I see the word* speed. *The* **s** *and the* **p** *make the* **sp** *sound and the two* **e's** *make the* **ee** *sound. What letter makes the* **d** *sound at the end of the word?*
- Introduce your child to tongue twisters. These are series of words that repeat the same sounds, which makes them difficult to say quickly. Your child should say the tongue twister slowly at first and focus on saying the vowels correctly. Then they should increase the speed at which they say them until their 'tongues' get 'twisted'.
- Use Dr Seuss books as these are an excellent way to learn vowel pronunciation.

This is because:

- Vowel sounds (the sounds made by the letters ***a***, ***e***, ***i***, ***o***, ***u***) are more difficult to hear than consonant sounds (the sounds made by the other letters of the alphabet) in words. Consonant sounds are usually written with only one letter, whereas vowel sounds are often written with combinations of letters that may include both vowels and consonants.
- Vowel sounds are more complex than consonant sounds. Children need to know that the same sound can be spelled with different letters (e.g. *n**o***, *kn**ow***, *d**oe***, and *d**ough***).
- Similarly, the same letter or letters can represent different sounds in different words, such as the letter ***o*** in *n**o**, t**o**, w**o**n* and *w**o**men* or the letters ***ow*** in *n**ow*** and *kn**ow***.
- The letter ***a*** has many sounds including the sounds of all the other vowels. Depending on its position in a word, ***a*** can sound like ***e***, ***i***, ***o*** and ***u***.
- By the age of seven, children should be able to hear the different sounds in words.

In a nutshell:

- Children need to know the difference between vowels and consonants.
- By age seven, children should be able to hear the different sounds in words.
- Children need to be able to tell you which letters are making a particular sound.
- Children need to know that the same letters can make different sounds and different letters can make the same sounds.

If your child cannot identify the words spoken by the characters in a story

Then:

They may not understand the significance of punctuation marks.

So, you can:

- Ask: *Tell me the words that [character name] actually said. How do you know this?*
- Draw the child's attention to the punctuation marks that indicate direct speech. Say: *You can tell that this is what [character name] is saying because the words have these marks around them. They are called speech marks or quotation marks and they enclose the spoken words of the characters in a book.*
- Say: *I want you to read the direct speech – the words spoken by the characters – and I will read the rest.*
- Choose a part of the book where two or more characters are conversing (if any); you take on the role of one character and your child takes the other role.
- If your child reads comic books, show them the role of speech and thought bubbles.

This is because:

- Knowing where the spoken words are enables children to distinguish between these and other words, which assists with comprehension.
- Children can practise expression and fluency with spoken language.
- Following a conversation makes reading more enjoyable.
- Dialogue is a large part of many early reading books.

In a nutshell:

- Direct speech is easy to identify if children are shown the punctuation marks that indicate it.
- Paying attention to the direct speech and reading it appropriately assists with comprehension and fluency.
- Being able to follow dialogue makes reading more enjoyable for children.

If your child cannot retell the main events of a story

Then:

They may be concentrating on what the words say rather than what the story is about.

So, you can:

- Tell them prior to reading that you will be asking them to retell the main events of the story. For example: *You are reading this to … . When you have finished reading this section, I want you to tell me … .*
- Draw attention to words that indicate sequence: *once upon a time, later that day, meanwhile, as soon as, next, up until now*, and so on.
- Say you will help them if they get stuck or forget.
- Remind them that it is OK to look at the book when they are retelling – some children think that a retell is a memory test; it isn't.
- Let them hold the book.
- Prompt with questions such as: *What do you remember? What else do you remember? What happened first? What happened after that? What happened before … ?*
- Reread the book at least once before the retelling.
- Prompt with sentence starters which they have to finish: *The children went to … . They did this because … .*

This is because:

- We always need a purpose for reading and reading is more effective if we know the purpose before reading.
- Children should be able to use the book to prompt them in their retell. It is important that children get the message that a book is something that you return to many times depending on your purpose.
- Children cannot be expected to decode, make meaning and remember at the same time. It is too much.
- Children reading aloud will be concentrating on how they sound and trying not to make mistakes. If you are going to ask them about their reading, they must be forewarned.

In a nutshell:

- Retelling the main events of a story is an important skill that shows comprehension.
- The book should always be there for reference during the retell if the child needs it.
- Always give a clear purpose for reading.

If your child cannot tell you why things happen in the texts that they read

Then:

They may not understand the relationship between cause and effect; this is common in children.

So, you can:

- Ask: *What happened?* (effect) *Why did it happen?* (cause)
- Look for the language of cause and effect (cause/effect linking words) and tell children that this language indicates that something is happening because of something else. It will be words such as *because, caused by, the result of, so, therefore, consequently*.
- Talk about everyday examples. For example: *I went to the dentist* (effect) *because* (cause/effect linking word) *my tooth hurt* (cause). *Dad's car broke down* (cause); *therefore* (cause/effect linking word), *I was late for school* (effect).

This is because:

- Understanding cause/effect relationships is a challenge for many children, yet it is a necessary skill because in school they are often asked to explain something.
- Words such as *because, caused by, the result of, so, therefore* and *consequently* set up the relationships between ideas in text, so are important.

In a nutshell:

- Children need to understand cause and effect.
- Alert children to the language of cause and effect.
- Use everyday examples to assist children to recognise what happens (effect) and why it happens (cause).

If your child decodes a word by saying the letters rather than the sounds made by the letters

Then:

They may not know the sounds that letters make or realise that letters have both a name and a sound.

So, you can:

- Ask: *Is saying the letters helping you work out the word?*
- Make sure your child can name every letter of the alphabet.
- Make sure they can distinguish between vowels and consonants.
- Teach the sounds that letters make individually and in combination. For example: *What sound does* **t-i-o-n** *make in* station*?* (shun).
- Talk to your child's teacher and ask if they have any activities that your child can do to learn the sounds made by the letters of the alphabet.
- Make up some letter cards and ask the child to say the letter name and letter sound or sounds.
- Use environmental print to draw attention to letters and sounds (e.g. McDonald's). Ask the child to name the beginning letter and the sound it makes.

This is because:

- Knowledge of letters and sounds (the alphabetical principle) is fundamental to reading.
- Children will not be able to decode quickly without this knowledge.

In a nutshell:

- Children need to know all the letters of the alphabet and which letters are vowels and which are consonants.
- Children also need to know the sounds letters make individually and in combination with other letters.
- Decoding is speeded up with this knowledge, allowing children to make sense of their reading.

See also, 'If your child cannot hear the vowel sounds in words or distinguish between the vowel and the consonant sounds' (page 24)

If your child does not appear to be advancing as quickly as others in the year level

Then:

They may have problems or they may be reading books at the same level to become more fluent and confident.

So, you can:

- Talk to your child's teacher and share your concerns. You can ask questions about your child's progress, the level of books they are reading and whether this is within the range of reasonable progress for their age.
- Avoid discussing your child's progress with other parents or comparing it with their child's progress. This is not especially helpful and can cause concern when it is not warranted.
- Avoid making comparisons with siblings or close family members – again, this is unlikely to be helpful.
- Keep reading *to*, *with* and *by* your child and creating opportunities for them to read.

This is because:

- Reading development is not a race to the finish.
- Some children make slower progress than others.
- Reading a variety of books at the same or an easier level is a good thing to do; it encourages accuracy, confidence and fluency.
- Early gains by some readers often level out as they move through the early years. However, an early small gap can become a large one very quickly, so ensure that you talk to your child's educators.

In a nutshell:

- Comparisons with other readers of the same age can harm more than help.
- Always talk to the child's teacher if you are concerned.
- Keep reading to your child and listening to them read.
- Children develop as readers at different rates, as they do in most areas.

If your child does not correct their own mistakes as they read (known as self-correction)

Then:

They are concentrating only on saying the words and not thinking about the meaning of the text.

So, you can:

- Give your child time to realise they have made a mistake and then correct it. Never interrupt a child's reading, when they are reading aloud, until they have had time to correct the mistake.
- At the end of the sentence/paragraph, say: *You said ... Did that make sense? Which was the tricky bit?*
- Encourage your child to say, *That didn't make sense*, and have another try.
- Go back to the start of the sentence and reread the sentence.
- Emphasise that reading must make sense and that the only reason we read is to make sense of what we read, so if reading does not make sense, then we need to have another try.
- Encourage them to build up a picture of what they are reading as they are reading (visualising).

This is because:

- If your child is not self-correcting, they are not monitoring their reading. Monitoring and self-correction are two vital reading behaviours.
- If children do not correct their own mistakes as they read, they are missing the critical point about why we read. **Reading must make sense.**
- We want readers to be independent and make their own decisions about what did and didn't make sense.

In a nutshell:

- Do not prompt until the reader has had time to self-correct.
- Monitoring and self-correction are vital reading behaviours that should be encouraged.
- Always say, *Did that make sense?* rather than, *That didn't make sense,* as this encourages the reader to take control of their reading.
- **Reading must make sense** and readers should expect reading to make sense.

If your child does not seem to know the sounds that letters make either on their own or in words

Then:	They are struggling to decode.
So, you can:	• Make sure your child can say all the letters of the alphabet. • Make sure they can identify which letters are consonants and which are vowels. • Make sure your child can give the sounds for each letter of the alphabet (initially one sound per letter, but later they can identify several sounds for the one letter). • Draw attention to words that begin or end with similar sounds. • Say, for example: Late *rhymes with* gate *and* date. *Can you think of any other words that rhyme with* late*?* • See if they can read nonsense words such as *bick*, *flep*, *tridding*, *tump*, *slar*, *vaz*, *frong*, and so on. There are lists of these words online which children can practise. • Talk about the fact that the same letter can make a different sound in different words. For example, *yellow*, *any* and *sky* show the three different sounds made by the letter *y*. • Introduce Spoonerisms – children can have fun changing beginning sounds of words. For example, *Rindercella, the girl who slopped her dripper* (Cinderella, the girl who dropped her slipper). • Seek help from your child's teacher or school principal.

This is because:

- While knowing letters and the sounds that letters make is not the only thing that makes a good reader, it is the first step and important that children learn this as soon as possible.
- If children do not have this knowledge well developed by age eight, they will struggle with reading.
- Rapid, accurate and efficient decoding frees up energy to make meaning.

In a nutshell:

- Children must know the names of the letters of the alphabet and the sounds these letters make.
- Children must know that the same letter can make a different sound in different words.
- Children must be able to make links between words (e.g. hear similar beginning sounds, end sounds and rhymes).

If your child gets in a mess, becomes confused, loses their way in the reading or everything falls apart and breaks down

Then:	They need a few minutes to regroup.
So, you can:	• Say: *Let's go back to the start of the sentence and have another try.* • Say: *Where was the tricky part? Look closely at this part … read it … now try from the beginning of the sentence.* • Say: *I'm going to be there if you need me to help you read through the tricky parts. I'll only cut in if I think you need me to.* • Say: *How about I read this part and you follow along? You can join in when you're ready.* • Say: *Let's have a break for a couple of minutes and come back to the reading.*
This is because:	• It's easy to be discouraged when reading becomes difficult. • Frustration is the enemy of all learning. • It's important that your child's reading experiences are positive and pleasurable, so they are happy to continue reading.
In a nutshell:	• Take time out. • Help your child by reading with them. • Keep all reading experiences positive and frustration to a minimum.

If your child has trouble identifying the main idea or point of the text

Then:

Do not be too concerned as this is a difficult skill, especially for young children.

So, you can:

- Talk about the difference between main ideas and details.
- Tell the child before they begin reading that you will be asking them to tell you what the main ideas are.
- Give them a point taken from the text and ask them to say whether they think it's a main idea or a detail.
- Say: *In no more than 30 words, I want you to tell me the main idea of the text.*
- Ask: *Which of these statements is best for the main idea of the text?*
- Encourage them to build up a picture of (visualise) what they are reading about.
- Ask: *Do you think this is an important point? Why/Why not?*

This is because:

- Children find it difficult to identify the main idea of a text. This is an essential skill for summarising and they need a great deal of help with it.
- Children often fixate on details. The ability to generalise is developmental and does not happen readily until the teenage years.
- Limiting the number of words forces children to think about the main idea.

In a nutshell:

- Introduce children to main ideas and details at a young age.
- Help them recognise main ideas and details by supporting them.
- Giving the purpose of identifying the main ideas before reading assists with identifying the main ideas.

If your child hesitates at a word

Then:

They may not know the word, may have forgotten the word or may have heard it but not recognise it in print.

So, you can:

- Be patient and wait while the child tries to work out the word. Curb your natural instinct to come to their aid too quickly.
- Offer some prompts: *Look at the picture for a clue. Are there any letters and sounds in the word that are familiar to you? What word would make sense here? Look at the beginning letters, do you know what sound they make? Get your mouth ready for the word.*
- Give a meaning (semantic) clue. For example: *Where do aeroplanes land?* (airport)
- Before frustration kicks in, tell them the word. Say: *I am going to tell you the word, then I want you to tell me how I know it is that word.* (There might be some familiar letter clusters or something in the picture that helps.)
- At the end of the reading, go back to the sentence with the tricky word and ask the child to reread it a couple of times. Ask: *Where was the tricky word? What are you going to do to help remember it for next time?*
- Teach the child to read through words where it doesn't matter if they can say them or not (e.g. names).

NB: The *sound it out* prompt is not always helpful and should not be the first prompt.

This is because:

- Your child may not have heard the word before.
- Reading is a problem-solving activity that takes time.
- There are many ways in which we can prompt children in their reading that are better than *sound it out*.
- Using a variety of prompts shows children that good readers do not rely on just one.

In a nutshell:

- Always wait – be patient.
- Always prompt – using a variety of prompts.
- Timing is of the essence – avoid frustration.
- Tell as a last resort.

If your child introduces anecdotes when reading and strays from the text
(e.g. They may talk about things unrelated to the text or with vague connections to it.)

Then:

They may be employing diversionary tactics to avoid reading, especially if they find reading difficult.

So, you can:

- Acknowledge that they have made a link with the text and tell the child that this is something good readers do.
- Draw them back to the text and focus on the reading.
- Say: *We'll talk about the book when we've finished reading. For now, stay focused on reading.*
- Say: *Read on … there might be more ways in which you can connect to the text.*
- Decide whether the talk is related in a meaningful way to the text or it is just for its own sake.

This is because:

- Some children become adept at avoiding reading by talking about things unrelated to the text.
- Discussion about reading is beneficial; it is what good readers do. However, discussion based on the reading is better than talking about unrelated things so as to avoid reading.
- Good readers give their complete attention to the reading task.

In a nutshell:

- Make sure talk about the text is related to it.
- Encourage the child to make links between the text and themselves and the text and the world.
- Discourage talking where it is occurring to avoid reading.
- Always allow some time to talk about the text after reading.
- Make links to books in your everyday activities.

If your child is a confident, competent reader

Then:

There is probably no need to listen to them read aloud very often. Good readers read every word, although it sometimes appears as if they don't.

So, you can:

- Talk about books with them.
- Provide them with a range of books from the library, especially different types of books on the same topic (e.g. a non-fiction book about frogs and a fiction book about frogs).
- Get them to read to younger siblings.
- Make connections between the texts they are reading and their lives. For example: *Is this like another book you have read? Has anything like this ever happened to you? Tell me about a time when …*

This is because:

- Reading aloud (in the early years of schooling) is something that is done so we can check children's progress. Once we are confident they can read well, there is really no need to listen to the child reading very often.
- Once children can read, they often prefer to read silently.
- Oral reading (reading aloud) is slower than silent reading (reading in your head). Once we can read, we find reading aloud too slow.
- However, reading aloud to others is a good chance to develop fluency and practise expression.
- It is a good idea for children to read different types of books. In preparation for the demands of high school, encourage children to read non-fiction as well as fiction.

In a nutshell:

- Even if children are confident, competent readers, talk to them about books and what they are reading.
- Encourage them to read a range of books and genres.
- Have them read aloud to younger siblings.

NB: It is generally not a good idea for a younger sibling who is a better reader to read to an older sibling who is a poorer reader. This may highlight the problem rather than help with the confidence of the poorer reader.

If your child is reluctant to read books

Then:

They may find the amount of text (i.e. words) too much.

So, you can:

- Do plenty of reading *with* – you do some, they do some.
- Break up the text into smaller, bite-sized pieces and gradually increase the amount of reading that is expected.
- Try other types of texts, especially those that contain plenty of information in visual form. Use high-interest magazines where the blocks of text tend to be shorter.
- Read to the 'sweet spot' of the story. This is the point at which the reader becomes hooked and wants to find out what is going to happen next. Your child may be curious and so prepared to read on.
- Use audiobooks to develop a love of reading. Listeners can enjoy the story without the difficulties associated with reading it themselves. Audiobooks with transcripts are the best as the listener can follow along.

This is because:

- Reading well is essential for life; it cannot be avoided. Without strong reading skills children may miss out on some of life's opportunities.
- Poor readers are usually poor writers and struggle with most aspects of schooling.

In a nutshell:

- Persist with encouraging your child to read.
- Share the reading – read *with*.
- Reduce large chunks of text to smaller pieces of reading that will be manageable.
- Try texts other than books.
- Read to the sweet spot of the story.
- Use audiobooks, preferably with transcripts.

If your child looks at the pictures for clues

Then:

They understand that a picture may give them a clue and help them read a word.

So, you can:

- Emphasise that good readers look at the pictures for clues, especially when they are stuck.
- Talk about what is in the pictures, especially before reading begins. Use them to introduce the storyline and the vocabulary, to predict what might happen and to encourage your child to practise some of the book's language prior to reading.
- If the child gets stuck on a word, ask: *What can you see in the picture to help you?*
- Praise the use of a picture: *I liked to way you looked at the picture when you got stuck. How did it help you with the word you didn't know?*

This is because:

- Caregivers often cover up pictures thinking that children are cheating when they use them.
- Good readers use information from many sources, including pictures.
- Pictures in early years reading books are included to support the written text.

In a nutshell:

- Don't cover up the pictures – they often provide clues to words.
- Talk about what is in the pictures, especially before reading begins.
- Reading is a problem-solving activity that needs clues from many sources.

If your child looks up at you every time they see a word they do not know or are not confident about

Then:

They are expecting you to tell them or confirm their guesses.

So, you can:

- Say: *Get your mouth ready for the word.*
- Pause – avoid telling as this is a last resort.
- Prompt: *Think about what would make sense. Is there a picture to help? Look at the beginning letters and sounds.* If this doesn't help, say: *Would ... fit here?*
- Remind them that it is their responsibility to have a go and you will help after they have thought about the word.
- Praise them when they have a go at the word, especially if their attempt makes sense. You might say: *Good try. You said ..., which makes sense, but let's have a look at it more closely. Have another go.*

This is because:

- Readers become reliant on others to tell them what the word is or if a mistake has been made and do not develop independence as readers.
- Reading is a problem-solving activity. It is not about being right the first time or indeed every time. Mistakes are part of reading. Even experienced and confident readers make errors.
- Readers who are not given the freedom to make mistakes and treat mistakes as part of their learning may develop negative attitudes to reading or lack confidence as readers.
- Habitual prompting by telling the words builds up a reader's expectation that difficulties will be resolved by the listener.

In a nutshell:

- Making mistakes is a healthy part of learning to read.
- Tell the word only as a last resort.
- Pause, Prompt and Praise every time.
- Ensure that any help you give is fostering the reader's independence.
- Readers need to rely on themselves not others.

If your child loses their place

Then:

They may not be monitoring meaning if they can't work out where they are (tracking). They may not realise that reading is more than just saying words.

So, you can:

- Say: *Follow with your eyes.*
- Place your finger (or ask the child to place their finger) in the margin next to the line being read rather than under each word.
- Hold a strip of clear plastic under the line.
- Ask: *How are you going to keep your place in future?*
- Help them to restart from where they lost their place.

This is because:

- Until they become more confident, quicker and more fluent readers, children may lose their place.
- Knowing where they are in their reading is an important skill for children to develop. Recognising that they have already read something and where they need to restart reading are important reading behaviours.

In a nutshell:

- Keeping track of where they are on the page is an important reading skill for children to learn.
- Finger pointing should be discouraged as it works again fluency, although a resting finger in the margin can help with tracking.
- A clear plastic guide held under the line can help.

If your child makes a mistake that affects meaning and does not realise it immediately

Then:

This is OK because we often need to read on to realise that we have made a mistake.

So, you can:

- Say nothing and wait – give the child time to realise they have made a mistake.
- If by the end of the sentence they have not realised the error, then say: *You said … Did that make sense? Let's go back and reread the sentence and think about what word would make sense here.* If they don't know, offer a suggestion: *Would … make sense?*

This is because:

- When we are reading, especially aloud, we make very rapid decisions about what we see and how we read what we see.
- Children must be given time to self-correct.
- They must be prompted if they are not able to correct the error, so that they can comprehend the text.
- A mistake that affects meaning is serious, especially if the child makes no effort to fix it up. It is a sign that the child is not monitoring or understanding what they are reading.

In a nutshell:

- Mistakes that affect meaning are serious ones.
- Always allow time for the child to self-correct.
- Tell as a last resort, but don't be afraid to tell. Often it keeps the reading moving.

If your child makes a mistake that does not affect meaning

(e.g. reads *home* for *house*, *lady* for *woman*, *bike* for *bicycle*)

Then:

They are monitoring the sense of their reading, and this is a good thing as they know that reading must make sense.

So, you can:

- Say nothing at the point of error (this is where the mistake is made).
- Let them finish reading to a point where there is a natural break (e.g. at the end of the sentence/paragraph).
- Say: *Let's look at this part again. You said [whatever they said]. That makes sense, but let's look at the word more closely. What is the word?* If the reader doesn't know, prompt with: *It's a word that means the same as [whatever they said].* If the reader still doesn't answer, tell them the word. *The word is ... Now you read this sentence again.*

This is because:

- Reading is a complex process. If the reader is thinking about meaning, they may make a mistake or momentarily fail to pay attention to the letter/sound information.
- Sometimes what they read is different from the printed text. This is acceptable if the meaning is not changed. If the reader self-corrects their mistake, praise them (e.g. *Good, now it makes sense*).
- Interrupting at the point of error is disruptive and can detract from the meaning-making process. It can make the reader fearful of being wrong and reluctant to try.
- Usually, having a second look at the word is enough for the child to read it correctly.

In a nutshell:

- Don't interrupt at the point of error as it disrupts the reading.
- Return to the word at a natural break in the reading.
- Prompt the reader so they can say the word correctly.
- Telling them the word is a last resort but sometimes is necessary.

If your child makes errors on more than 1 in 10 words

Then:

The text is too difficult for them and comprehension of the text will not occur.

So, you can:

- Talk about the text prior to reading. For example, if the text is about Ned Kelly, tell the child who he was, what he did and why some people think he was a hero/villain.
- Identify the difficult words prior to reading. Get the child to say the words after you have said them, and quickly tell them what they mean. This introduces the child to the words before they read, thus reducing cognitive load.
- Read them through the difficult parts. This means you read with them just a fraction behind them until there is a difficult part. Then you read a little ahead of them through the difficult part.
- If the child gets stuck while reading, continue reading to them.
- Choose easier texts on the same topic (see Appendix C).
- Put the text away until the child is in a better frame of mind, especially if they are becoming frustrated and cross.

This is because:

- Struggling with text is frustrating for many developing readers. They are much more likely to develop negative attitudes to reading if reading is not a pleasurable experience.
- Talking about the text and the vocabulary before reading occurs can help make decoding automatic, leaving more working memory available to think about meaning.

In a nutshell:

- Generally, text is too difficult if the reader makes errors on more than 1 in 10 words.
- Talk about the text before reading to reduce the difficulty of the text and build knowledge of the topic.
- Pre-teach the vocabulary – tell, don't ask, what words mean as this is quicker.
- Read along with your child to a greater or lesser extent depending on the difficulty of the text and the mood of the child.

If your child makes wild guesses at words based on the first couple of letters of the word

Then:

They are not thinking about the sense or meaning of the text, only the phonics.

So, you can:

- Avoid saying: *That's not right. It's … .*
- Instead, say: *You said … . Did that make sense/sound right?*
- Say: *Read the sentence again and think if the word … makes sense.*
- Ask: *What other word would make sense here? Have a look for some clues.*
- Ask: *Besides the letters, what else will help you to work out what the word is?*
- Tell the child the word as a last resort.

This is because:

- Readers who become fixated on letter sound patterns are not thinking about the other clues we use when we read. Good readers think about what makes sense and sounds right as well as looking at the letters and thinking about the sounds those letters make.
- Readers need to be in charge of their reading and encouraged to pick up their own mistakes.
- Reading is about making sense, so children need to be alerted to mistakes that don't make sense and do something about it.

In a nutshell:

- Sense making is everything.
- Good readers think about what makes sense and sounds right; they look at the letters and think about the sounds those letters make.
- Always ask questions of the reader as it forces them to think for themselves and increases their independence.

If your child moves their head as they read

Then:

They are not using their eyes as effectively as they should and may lose their place.

So, you can:

- Say: *Read it with your eyes and keep your head still.*
- Encourage them to practise looking at things without moving their head. For example, ask them to look at and between objects within range by moving their eyes rather than their head.
- Raise the book on a sloping surface (about 30 degrees).

This is because:

- Reading 'with your eyes' is quicker, more efficient and less tiring than reading by moving the head.
- A sloped surface improves the range of vision and encourages reading using eye movements.

In a nutshell:

- During reading eyes should move but not the head.
- Ask the child to practise moving their eyes while keeping their head still.
- Raise the book on a sloping surface.

If your child points to the words with their finger as they read

Then:

They see reading as an activity of calling words or 'barking at print' rather than making meaning.

So, you can:

- Tell them to read with their eyes.
- Show them how good readers look ahead and as they are saying a word, their eyes are looking at the next word or words. The better we get at this the further ahead we look.
- Place a piece of clear plastic under the line being read so the child will not lose their place but can see ahead through the plastic. It is important that the line being read is visible (obviously!) as well as the first three to four words of the next line.

This is because:

- In the long term, finger pointing limits fluency and so should be discouraged.
- Reading words individually rather than in phrases also works against fluent reading.
- Reading words individually sends the wrong message about reading as it suggests that reading is word calling only and not for making meaning.

In a nutshell:

- Discourage finger pointing.
- Tell your child to read the text with their eyes not their fingers.
- Use clear plastic to guide the reader.

NB: Finger pointing is something that beginning readers do. We need to discourage finger pointing from approximately eight years of age.

If your child reads accurately but very slowly

Then:

They need to develop fluency.

So, you can:

- Read with them and speed things up.
- Ask them to read the text several times as this will improve the speed at which they recognise words, allowing them time to concentrate on fluency.
- Ask them to practise a small part of the text – one page or one paragraph – until they can read it smoothly. It's worth saying that anything worth reading is worth reading several times.
- Model phrasing, that is, reading words in chunks or phrases rather than individually.
- Ask them to practise phrasing with just one or two sentences.
- Initially choose books with more natural language (language of speech) rather than books where the language is unfamiliar (technical, old fashioned, from different cultures, stilted or unlike speaking).
- Ensure the reader has rapid recall of the 200 most common words in English (see Appendix D).

This is because:

- Once word recognition becomes automatic, readers can concentrate on how they sound and develop fluency.
- Practice makes perfect so practising sections of text helps the developing reader.
- It is difficult to make meaning if we are not fluent.

In a nutshell:

- Fluency is essential for making meaning.
- Practise reading familiar texts – read the same text several times.
- Model reading behaviours so that your child knows what you mean.
- Choose books with more natural language.
- Practise reading high-frequency words.

If your child reads (i.e. decodes) accurately but has no idea what they have read when you ask questions after the reading

Then:	They are putting all their energy into saying the words accurately and thinking more about being error free than making meaning.
So, you can:	• Read the questions **before** reading the text if the purpose of reading is to answer questions. • Say: *As you read this story, I want you to look/listen for, think about, keep in mind, be able to tell me ... and we'll talk about that after you have read.* This is giving a purpose for reading, which gives the reader something to focus on. • Introduce the idea of keywords – these are words in the text that relate to its main topic. • Reread the text several times with the questions in mind. Say: *You can read the text again and this time look for ...* • Emphasise that the only reason we read anything is to make sense of it, and this is more important than just being able to say the words.
This is because:	• We often think that the reader who says every word accurately has some idea about what they have read, but this is not necessarily the case. • Rereading improves fluency but also makes for greater automaticity. This frees up cognitive space to think about the meaning of text as it is being read. • Decoding may take all the child's cognitive effort so there is nothing left to think about meaning. • When we read aloud, we worry more about how we sound or whether we will make a mistake than we do about what the text is about.

In a nutshell:

- Don't be fooled – word-perfect decoding is no indication that comprehension is occurring.
- Alert the reader to the purpose for reading before reading begins. If there are questions, show them to the child before reading.
- Reread the text several times to improve fluency and automaticity.

If your child reads in a monotone

Then:

The text may be too difficult. The child may not realise that reading aloud requires expression or they may be concentrating on the words.

So, you can:

- Model reading in an engaging and dynamic voice.
- Get your child to copy you.
- Choose a part of the book that has dialogue (conversation between two or more characters) and you read the lines of one character and your child the lines of another.
- In everyday conversation, ask your child to speak in various voices (excited, angry, secretive, and so on).
- Ask your child to reread a small part of the text with expression.

This is because:

- While there are not many places (other than school) where reading aloud is practised, when it is, it should engage the listener.
- Reading aloud with expression is linked to fluent reading – one tends to make the other possible.

In a nutshell:

- Reading aloud should engage the listener.
- Model how reading aloud should sound.
- Have your child copy the way you read with expression.

If your child reads slowly in a laboured way

Then:

The text is probably too difficult for them.

So, you can:

- Find an easier text (see Appendix C). As a general rule, text is too difficult for readers if they stumble on more than 1 in 10 words (approximately 10%).
- Make sure they know the 200 most common words in English (see Appendix D). Children should learn these as quickly as possible because they make up approximately 80% of all English sentences.
- Read the text with the child, keeping a little behind them and carrying them through the 'tricky' parts.
- Read the text and ask your child to follow with their eyes. Do this a couple of times, then get your child to read the text, prompting and 'reading with' if necessary.
- Use text-to-speech software and let the child listen to the text a couple of times before they read it. (Electronic devices have this function and there are plenty of programs on the internet.)
- Encourage reading of the text several times to improve fluency.

This is because:

- Reading slowly in a laboured way is generally a sign that the text is too difficult for the reader. The reader is putting all their energy into 'saying' the words (decoding), leaving very little room for the brain to make meaning.
- Readers who do not become fluent (i.e. read quickly and smoothly) become discouraged and so do less of the very thing they should do more of to become better (i.e. reading).
- Rapid, accurate and efficient decoding of text is essential before comprehension can occur. If decoding is slow and inaccurate, nothing much else is happening in the reading process.

In a nutshell:

- Check text difficulty.
- Help the reader learn the 200 most common words in English.
- Read with your child.
- Obtain text-to-speech software.
- Encourage several readings to improve fluency.

If your child reads through or ignores punctuation and does not realise that what they have read doesn't make sense

Then:

They are focusing on the words and ignoring the punctuation.

So, you can:

- Talk about the punctuation in the text prior to reading and the role it plays. For example: *This is a full stop and it means that we pause slightly before we start reading again.*
- Ask your child to reread the text – this time paying attention to the punctuation marks.
- Explain that punctuation does matter – compare 'Let's eat Grandma!' with 'Let's eat, Grandma!'
- Encourage rereading of a sentence; the second time, focus on the punctuation used.
- Encourage phrasing (reading in meaningful chunks).
- Encourage pausing at full stops and commas.

This is because:

- Most punctuation marks are very small and easily overlooked by children.
- Punctuation enables us to make sense of what we read. Changing or omitting punctuation marks can affect the meaning the reader makes of the text.
- Punctuation also helps with phrasing and fluency.

In a nutshell:

- Punctuation is important and assists with making meaning.
- Draw attention to punctuation marks and their roles.
- Rereading text several times allows children to focus on the punctuation.

If your child reads very quickly

Then:

This is not an issue unless they are not comprehending what they have read. If they are reading to an audience, though, fast reading may not help the listener understand what is being read.

So, you can:

- Ask them to retell the reading in their own words. This will enable you to see if they have understood what they have read.
- Ask them to reread part of the text more slowly and with expression. Tell them they are reading to entertain a listener.
- Model reading aloud with fluency and expression rather than just speed.

This is because:

- Reading quickly, especially when reading aloud, can interfere with comprehension.
- The pace of reading should be adjusted according to the audience and/or purpose for reading.
- Reading quickly can convey the message that reading is about 'saying the words' not making meaning.
- It may be a sign that your child sees reading as a chore and something to be done and got out of the way quickly.

In a nutshell:

- Fast reading is not a problem as long as readers are making meaning.
- Model reading aloud at a more moderate pace.
- The pace of reading is determined by the audience and/or purpose for the reading.
- Do not always discourage fast reading. Most reading is done 'in the head', so fast reading can be a good thing.
- If you are confident that your child is a good reader then leave it at that.

If your child reads word by word without fluency

Then:	It is unlikely they will be making meaning from the text.
So, you can:	• Encourage them to see words in groups (phrases) rather than individually. • Show them how to move their eyes ahead, particularly when moving to the next line. Focus on the second or third word of the new line – their eyes will see and the brain will register the first one or two words. • Encourage several readings so that fluency can be practised – read along with them for some of these readings.
This is because:	• Reading word by word is not pleasurable for the reader (or the listener). • Lack of fluency inhibits comprehension because the reader is likely to be focusing on decoding and saying the words rather than on their meaning. • Good readers let their eyes move ahead so they are ready for the words that are coming up and they can get their mouths ready to say them.
In a nutshell:	• Few readers enjoy reading word by word. • Rereading improves fluency and therefore comprehension. • As good readers read, their eyes have moved ahead of the words they are reading. This promotes fluency.

See also, 'If your child reads slowly in a laboured way' (page 60), which has more suggestions for this type of problem.

If your child shows no interest in reading

Then:

Reading may be difficult for them; they may find other pursuits more enjoyable; the texts may be too long.

So, you can:

- Encourage your child to read anything and everything, especially longer pieces of writing.
- Value and model reading in the home. Try 'screen-free time' where everyone reads.
- Find out from librarians the types of books that young people are reading.
- Use high-interest texts such as magazines where the blocks of text tend to be shorter.
- Read with your child, especially during homework sessions.
- Keep reading sessions short (10–15 minutes) and frequent.
- For boys especially, encourage the male members of your family and friends to talk about the value of reading to them and why it is important to be a confident and competent reader.
- Listen to audiobooks, especially those with transcripts.
- Use a sports analogy – to be successful at sport, you must practice; to be successful in school and life, you must be able to read.

This is because:

- Reading well is essential for life; it cannot be avoided. Without strong reading skills children may miss out on some of life's opportunities.
- Poor readers are usually poor writers and struggle with most aspects of schooling.

In a nutshell:

- Children must read and caregivers must do all in their power to make this happen.
- Read short texts, read frequently and keep the sessions short.
- Include screen-free time in your home routine and model and value reading.
- Use electronic resources to reduce the demands of reading.
- Use a sports analogy to encourage reading.

If your child sounds out a word letter by letter

Then:

They may have learnt that this is something they should do, even though it is not always the most effective strategy for decoding words.

So, you can:

- Break up words into chunks or syllables instead. For example, the word *window* can be split into two syllables, *win* and *dow*.
- Look for letter combinations in words that are familiar to the child (e.g. *an, sh, en*).
- Talk about the number of separate sounds in words (phonemes).
- Clap the number of syllables or separate sounds in the word. For older children, use chin drops instead of claps. Ask them to place a couple of fingers lightly on their chin and say the word. They should be able to feel the chin drop with each syllable.

This is because:

- If the child hasn't heard a word before, then breaking it up into individual letter sounds is not the most useful strategy to decode it.
- A more effective strategy is to chunk letters into syllables so the child learns that most words are made up of letters grouped into single sounds. For example, the word *separate* is made up of three sounds: *sep-a-rate*. When reading, children need to see and hear the clusters of letters that make the sounds rather than individual letter sounds.
- The main reason for children to know the individual letter sounds is that this helps with identifying the sounds syllables make.

In a nutshell:

- When faced with an unfamiliar word, break it into chunks or syllables rather than letters.
- Look for familiar letter combinations.
- Help children to identify the sounds or syllables in a word by clapping or using chin drops.

If your child stops reading to ask what a word means

Then:

They are monitoring their reading and realise that they need to know what the word means so they can make sense of their reading.

So, you can:

- Ask them to think about the use of the word in the text. Say: *Let's look where the word is in the sentence and what the surrounding text is about.*
- Say: *See if you can guess at the end of the sentence.*
- Ask: *Is it like any word you know?*
- Give them a couple of meanings to choose from and ask them to think which makes more sense. For example: *The boy ambled to school. Do you think* ambled *means moved quickly or walked slowly?*
- Avoid getting out the dictionary yet – this disrupts the reading and is too slow for most children.
- Look up the word together after the reading and then go back and see how it is used in the sentence.
- Tell them quickly so that the reading is not disrupted.

This is because:

- During reading time, the child should focus on the reading and not be distracted by other things.
- Giving children a choice of meanings forces them to think about the best fit for sense making.
- Encouraging children to be interested in words and be curious about what words mean builds their vocabulary, and this assists with reading development.

In a nutshell:

- Stay focused on reading.
- Encourage children's interest in words.
- Give children meanings to choose from as this causes them to think about the text.

If your child struggles with the pronunciation of words

Then:

They have probably not heard or seen the words before or may recognise them when they hear them and not make the link between how the word looks in print and how it sounds.

So, you can:

- Pronounce the word for them and get them to repeat it with you and then on their own. Say: *I'll say the word … . Now let's say it together … . Now you say it on your own.*
- Break up the word into syllables (e.g. *dif/fer/ent*).
- Draw attention to words that have the same letter sounds but different spellings (e.g. *s**oo**n*, ***f**l**ew***, *cl**ue***). Say: *Parts of these words sound the same but see how they are spelled differently.* This helps with spelling as well as pronunciation.
- Choose books where the language is more like speaking (natural language) rather than books where the language is unfamiliar (technical, old fashioned, from different cultures, stilted or very unlike speaking).

This is because:

- Readers become much more confident about reading words they can pronounce. We tend to avoid using words whose pronunciation we find challenging.
- As children move through school, they encounter many new and unfamiliar words, especially in high school texts, so need to be confident with pronunciation.
- Writers need to make choices when spelling words because some words sound similar but have different spelling patterns.

In a nutshell:

- The ability to pronounce words gives readers confidence.
- Breaking up words into syllables helps with pronunciation.
- Correct pronunciation helps with spelling.
- Choose books with natural language.

If your child struggles with their home readers

Then:

The books may be unfamiliar and too difficult. If your child is making mistakes on more than 1 in 10 words (10%), then the text is challenging.

So, you can:

- Let the child's teacher know.
- Read the book through a couple of times to the child and get them to follow along as you read.
- Ask the child to read the book or part of it after you have read it through.
- Choose a book from the child's own library so they at least do some reading.

This is because:

- Home reading (especially of books that are sent home from school) should be an opportunity to practise reading strategies on familiar texts.
- If the book is too difficult, the teacher must be informed.
- The excuse of a book being too difficult should not be used to avoid reading.

In a nutshell:

- Home readers are for practising reading on familiar texts.
- The teacher is the best person to control book choice.
- Children, especially strugglers, become good at avoiding reading; they must not be allowed to do this.

If your child tries to read a book about which they know very little

Then:

They probably haven't given a great deal of thought to their book selection or they may have been attracted by something on the cover or be interested in the topic.

So, you can:

- Google some images of the topic. For example, if the book is on the Olympic Games show them some images of the Games.
- Give them some background knowledge and use some of the words they will encounter in the book.
- 'Walk' through the book to increase familiarity with the topic. You can give information and ask questions to ascertain what your child knows.
- Talk about what the book is about without taking away the purpose for reading (i.e. don't tell them what is in the book).
- Give them a purpose for reading. Say: *As you read the book, I want you to find out about … , to see what happens when … , to see if … , to look for the reasons for …* , and so on.

This is because:

- Children often select books based on the cover but may not have any background or vocabulary knowledge to make reading it possible.
- Bringing unfamiliar material home is not a problem, but children will need a knowledge base on which to lay the new material.
- Children should be encouraged to read widely.

In a nutshell:

- Talking about books prior to reading helps children to make sense of the book even if the content is unfamiliar.
- Give children a purpose for reading the book.
- Encourage children to read widely.
- Children are often more motivated to read books they have selected themselves.

Handy tips for vocabulary and spelling development

Vocabulary development

Tip 1: Play word games

Encourage an interest in words by playing word games with your children. A good game to play in the car is to start with a word, then each person in the car has to make a new word by changing one letter in the word. For example, if the first word is *pig*, the second one could be *dig*, followed by *dog*, *dot*, *pot*, *pit*, and so on.

Another easy game to play is one where clues are revealed one by one. For example:

> *I am thinking of a word that has four letters.*
>
> *The word is something that has seven things in it.*
>
> *It rhymes with creek.*
>
> *The first letter is* **w** *which makes a* **wu** *sound.*
>
> *Can you guess the word?*
>
> ANSWER: week

Tip 2: Use more sophisticated words in speech

When speaking to your child, use more sophisticated words for concepts that children understand. For example, a child might describe a piece of fruit as *yucky* because it has gone black or has mould on it. You can say: *The fruit is discoloured or too ripe. It's inedible so we can't eat it.* You will find that when you think about this practice, it will come more naturally to you.

Tip 3: Link the spoken and written word

Make the link between the spoken word and the written word. Use butcher's paper as a tablecloth and leave a few marker pens on the table. Once the meal is over and as you are talking about the day's events, you can write a few words down when they come up in conversation. Over a few days, there will be lots of words and children will be able to connect with them.

Tip 4: Offer replacements for overused words

When children overuse certain words and phrases (e.g. *nice, said, got, a lot of, and then*), which they tend to do in speaking and writing, we often say, *Can you think of a better word than ... ?* If they could have, wouldn't they have used it? A better approach is to say, *Here are a couple of words you could use instead of ... ; choose one.*

Handy tips for vocabulary and spelling development

Tip 5: Label items around the home

Label items in the house. This will make your home look like a classroom for a few years, but it's well worth it as it helps children with word recognition.

Tip 6: Pre-teach new vocabulary before reading

Always pre-teach new vocabulary before reading if the book is an unfamiliar one. The following routine is helpful:

> *Once there lived a wolf in the jungle. The wolf was hungry for many days and was growing weaker day by day.*
>
> Listener (L), Child (Ch)
>
> L: *Can you point to the word on the first line that means a lot of trees and plants in a hot place?*
>
> Wait for the child to identify *jungle*.
>
> L: *You should have your finger on* jungle. *(If they haven't, they can move it there.)*
>
> L: *I'll say* jungle, *now you say* jungle.
>
> Ch: *Jungle.*
>
> Child repeats the word if it is a difficult one.
>
> L: *Can you tell me what a jungle is?*
>
> Ch: *It's a hot place where there are trees and plants.*
>
> L: *Yes. Now let's look at another word.*

NB:

- Ensure the definitions are short and simple and do not contain other words that need explanation.
- If there are a lot of unfamiliar words, it's a good idea to break the reading into sections and pre-teach three to five words before each section.
- You choose the words. When asked if there are any words they don't know, children often don't know what they don't know so are unable to identify these words.

Tip 7: Draw attention to words in the same family

When talking about words, draw attention to words in the same family. Word families contain words that are similar in form and meaning. For example, *swim, swimming, swam, swum, swimmer*.

Tip 8: Create a vocabulary chart

Create an alphabet vocabulary chart and as children learn new words, they can write them in the correct place.

Alphabet vocabulary chart

a-b	c-d	e-f
g-h	i-j	k-l
m-n	o-p	q-r
s-t	u-v-w	x-y-z

Tip 9: Use body language and movement

Use body language and movement to illustrate the meanings of words. For example, walk quickly and say to your child, *I am walking speedily/rapidly/with great haste* (choose one) to illustrate the word. Use facial expressions to illustrate words, for example, *I am listening intently* (facial expression is one of concentration).

Tip 10: Discuss the different meanings of words

Many words in the English language have several meanings. Discuss the different meanings of words with children.

Example: **pitch**

> '**Pitch** the ball low and straight,' screamed the baseball coach. (*pitch* as a verb meaning to throw)
>
> The cricket **pitch** was damaged during the recent hailstorm and the groundkeeper said it was unplayable. (*pitch* as a noun meaning the area between the wickets in cricket)
>
> 'It's **pitch**-black outside,' warned Dad. 'Make sure you take a powerful torch.' (*pitch* as an adjective meaning very black or dark)

Spelling development – reading

Children who read well are often good spellers. This is because spelling and reading are closely linked. They involve the relationship between letters and sounds. Learning to spell and learning to read occur in shared areas of the brain that build links between the visual form (the look of a word) and the auditory form (the sounds of a word). Spelling is *encoding* words by retrieving from the brain the letters that make sounds and putting these letters together to make words. Reading is *decoding* words by retrieving the same information needed to spell.

Children's reading development is accelerated if caregivers draw attention to the spelling of words *before* and *after* reading. Talking about the spelling of words *during* reading is not a good idea as it slows down reading and can interfere with fluency.

Spelling knowledge that children gain as they read helps their development as writers.

Tip 1: Break words into syllables

Before children begin reading, choose three or four words from the text that they may not know. For each word, say: *I'll say the word … . Now let's say it together. I'm going to clap the number of syllables (separate sounds in the word) and I want you to tell me how many syllables you hear.*

NB: Asking children to identify words they don't know is problematic because they often don't know what they don't know. Sometimes they know a word when they hear it but do not recognise it in print. For this activity, it is better if the caregiver chooses the words.

Tip 2: Beginning, middle and end sounds or syllables

Before reading or after children have read, choose three or four words from the text. These can be familiar or unfamiliar words. Say: *I'll say the word … . Now let's say it together … . Now you say it on your own.*

Then say: *I'll say one of the sounds or syllables in the word and you can tell me if the sound is from the beginning, middle or end of the word.*

Example

Say: *This word is* elephant. *Say it with me* [elephant]. *Now say it on your own* [elephant]. *Listen to the sound I say and tell me where in the word you can hear that sound. Where is the sound* **phant**? *Is that a beginning, middle or end sound?* [end] *Where do you hear* **le** *in the word* elephant? [middle].

NB: For early readers, beginning and end sounds are easier to hear than middle sounds. If children find this challenging, you may need to add a step after the child has pronounced the word. Say: *I'll say the beginning sound … . Now let's say it together … . Now you say it on your own.*

Do this for beginning, middle and end sounds until the child can do this independently.

Tip 3: Same sounds, different spellings and same spellings, different sounds

After the child has read the text, spend a few minutes studying some of the words they have read. Look for examples and talk about words that have the same letter sounds but are spelled differently (e.g. *s**oo**n, fl**ew**, cl**ue***). Say: *Parts of these words sound the same, but see how they are spelled differently?* This helps with reading, pronunciation and spelling.

You can also point out or ask children to find words or parts of words with the same spelling that are pronounced differently. Say: *Look at these letters,* **o-u-g-h**. *In* rough, *they make an* **uff** *sound but in* cough, *they make an* **off** *sound, in* dough, *they make an* **o** *sound and in* plough, *they make an* **ow** *sound. I'm going to say some other* **o-u-g-h** *words. Tell me the sound that you hear in the word.*

Tip 4: Encourage children to find misspelled words

Encourage children to identify misspelled words themselves, although this can be difficult for them. To identify a misspelled word, you have to know how to spell it, and they may not know. Use environmental print in your local area and encourage children to look for misspelled words.

Tip 5: Teach some spelling rules and their exceptions

Spelling rules such as '***i*** before ***e*** except after ***c***' work in about 85% of cases, so they are worth learning. The exceptions to the rules are also worth learning. For example, the '***i*** before ***e*** except after ***c***' rule generally only applies to words with a long **ee** sound (e.g. *believe, achieve, chief, piece, receive, perceive, ceiling*) and not to those with an ***ay*** sound (e.g. *neighbour, weigh, eight, vein*).

NB: When teaching spelling rules, apply them to words that students are reading.

Tip 6: Devise activities for children to interact with the spelling of words

Most children have weekly spelling lists, especially in the primary years. One of the problems with this approach is that words learnt in lists tend to be remembered in lists. It can be frustrating when children are unable to transfer the correct spelling of a word (in their weekly test) to their writing. Children need to interact more with the spelling of the words in the list. The following table provides some ideas for doing this.

Handy tips for vocabulary and spelling development

Activity		Example
1.	Break the word into syllables using a solidus (/).	*break/fast*
2.	Break the word into its root word plus affixes (i.e. prefixes and suffixes).	*dis-appear-ance* (*dis* = prefix, *appear* = root word, *ance* = suffix)
3.	Use a mnemonic (memory trick) to help with the spelling of a word.	*station**e**ry* – the **e** in *station**e**ry* reminds me of envelopes, so I know that this is the way to spell the word when referring to pens, papers, envelopes, etc.
4.	Say the word exactly as it is spelled.	*li … bra … ry, Feb … ru … a … ry*
5.	Notice little words in big words.	*par* in *se**par**ate*
6.	Identify the 'tricky bit' of the word and devise a way to remember how to spell this part.	The 'tricky bit' in *their* are the letters ***ei***. Remember that **e** comes before ***i*** in the alphabet.
7.	Spell other words related to the word.	If the spelling word is *please*, spell *pleasant, pleased, pleasing, unpleasant, unpleasantly*.
8.	Write out the words with one small error in each word. Ask your child to identify the error and write the word correctly, using their list if necessary.	*yelow* – missing *l*; correct spelling *yellow*
9.	Practise *Look, Cover, Say, Write* and *Check*.	*Look* at the word *Cover* it up *Say* it aloud a couple of times and visualise it *Write* the word *Check* the spelling by removing the cover
10.	Write the words in alphabetical order.	*city, farm, house, paddock, river, road*

Spelling development – writing

Caregivers often need to help children with their writing as well as their reading, so here are a few useful spelling tips focussed on writing.

Tip 1: Avoid pointing out errors during writing

Avoid pointing out spelling errors as children write. Writing is a complex task, and the writer has many things to think about as they write. Drawing attention to spelling errors during the writing process will disrupt the flow of ideas and may make the writer reluctant to use words because they are unsure how to spell them. They will keep using familiar words rather than experiment with new ones. Correcting spelling is part of the proofreading phase of writing, not the composing phase.

Tip 2: Respond if the child asks how to spell a word

If a child asks you how to spell a word as they are writing, you can try the following responses:

- Say: *Have a go – we can correct it later.*
- Tell them how to spell it. This is quick and does not disrupt the writing process. After they have finished writing, you can ask them how they will remember how to spell the word.
- Stretch out the word and see if this helps the child spell each syllable.

NB: This is not the time to refer to a dictionary. Using a dictionary can be tedious (especially if the child does not have dictionary skills) and may stop the reluctant writer from returning to the writing.

Tip 3: Don't correct all spelling errors if there are many

If the child has made many spelling errors, do not attempt to correct every one. You can say: *You have some words spelled incorrectly – we're just going to focus on a couple of them today.*

You could focus on keywords, commonly misspelled words or sight words.

Appendices

Appendix A: Prompts to help children read unknown words

If children become stuck on a word when reading, try the following prompts:

Break the word into syllables or smaller pieces.

Look at the beginning letter/s of the word and think about the sounds it/ they make – get your mouth ready to say it/them.

Look at how the word ends. Is that a familiar ending to you?

Look at the picture.

What do you think it might be?

Have a go.

Read on to the end of the sentence then try reading the sentence again.

Use the prefixes and suffixes.

Can you see a small word in the word?

Can you find the word or letter anywhere in the room?

Does it make sense?

Is the word similar to other words you know?

Do you know another word that looks like this word?

Does that make sense? Have another go and think about the sense of what you are reading.

Good try, but look closer at the word.

Read the next sentence and then come back.

Would you speak like that?

This is a sight word.

The word rhymes with … (e.g. *bat* for *flat*).

Appendix A

At the end of the page or paragraph, ask:

You said …; did that sound right?

You said …; did that make sense?

Where was the tricky bit?

Does that look right?

Can we say it that way?

Did you have enough/too many words?

Appendix B: Comments to praise children for their reading behaviours

Praise specific reading behaviours to reinforce those behaviours. Struggling readers are often unable to monitor what they are doing wrong but are also unable to monitor what they are doing right. Avoid comments such as, *You read really well today* or *That's great reading, well done!* as these are not specific enough and do not focus on particular reading behaviours. The comments below are focused and enable you to draw attention to what the reader is doing.

I liked the way you:

- *didn't find excuses to avoid reading.*
- *realised that you'd made a mistake and went back and fixed it up. That's self-correction and it's what good readers do.*
- *read smoothly and fluently in a speaking voice.*
- *read with expression.*
- *paused at the commas and full stops, and this helped you to make meaning from your reading.*
- *listened to yourself read and built up a picture of what you were reading.*
- *didn't give up even though there were some tricky parts.*
- *read in phrases.*
- *stopped when the reading didn't make sense.*
- *let your eyes move ahead so you could read smoothly.*
- *got your mouth ready for the word.*
- *worked the word out by looking for parts of the word you've seen before.*
- *read the story using a talking voice.*
- *remembered the words we learnt.*
- *worked very hard today so that your reading made sense. That's what good readers do and by doing that you are well on your way to becoming a good reader.*
- *happily reread the book.*
- *gave all your attention to reading today.*
- *used the strategy of ... which you've been learning.*
- *used clues from the pictures.*
- *changed your voice when you read the direct speech.*

- *no longer need your finger to keep your place.*
- *related what you read to something you know.*
- *retold the main events of the story.*
- *paid close attention to word endings.*
- *used my suggestions to help you.*
- *have learnt the 200 most common words.*
- *realised that the answer to the question was not 'right there'. You had to think about it.*
- *identified the main idea of the book.*
- *can name the vowels and the consonants.*
- *know most of the sounds the letters make.*

Appendix C: Levels of difficulty and readability

Levelled readers

These are a collection or set of books at different levels of difficulty from easiest to most challenging. There are many commercially produced sets of these levelled readers and you will probably find that your child's school uses one or more of them. Several factors are used to decide how easy or difficult a book is. These include length, layout, structure and organisation, illustrations, words, phrases and sentences, literary features, and content and theme.

Flesch–Kincaid readability tests

Microsoft Word provides useful tools for measuring text difficulty called the Flesch–Kincaid readability tests as well as other readability statistics. If children are downloading information from the internet for study purposes, it is important that it is easy enough for them to comprehend and use. They are more likely to copy text that is too difficult for them.

Follow these steps to turn on the Flesch–Kincaid and other readability statistics in Microsoft Word:

> Click File
>
> Scroll down, click Options
>
> Click Proofing
>
> Click Show readability statistics box (under the heading 'When correcting spelling and grammar in Word'). Click OK.
>
> Click the Review tab then Spelling & Grammar (or Editor in some versions of Word) to open the spelling and grammar check; a shortcut for this is the F7 key.
>
> Correct or ignore all errors found in the spelling and grammar check (you need to do this before the readability statistics will display).
>
> The Readability Statistics dialogue box will appear:

Appendix C

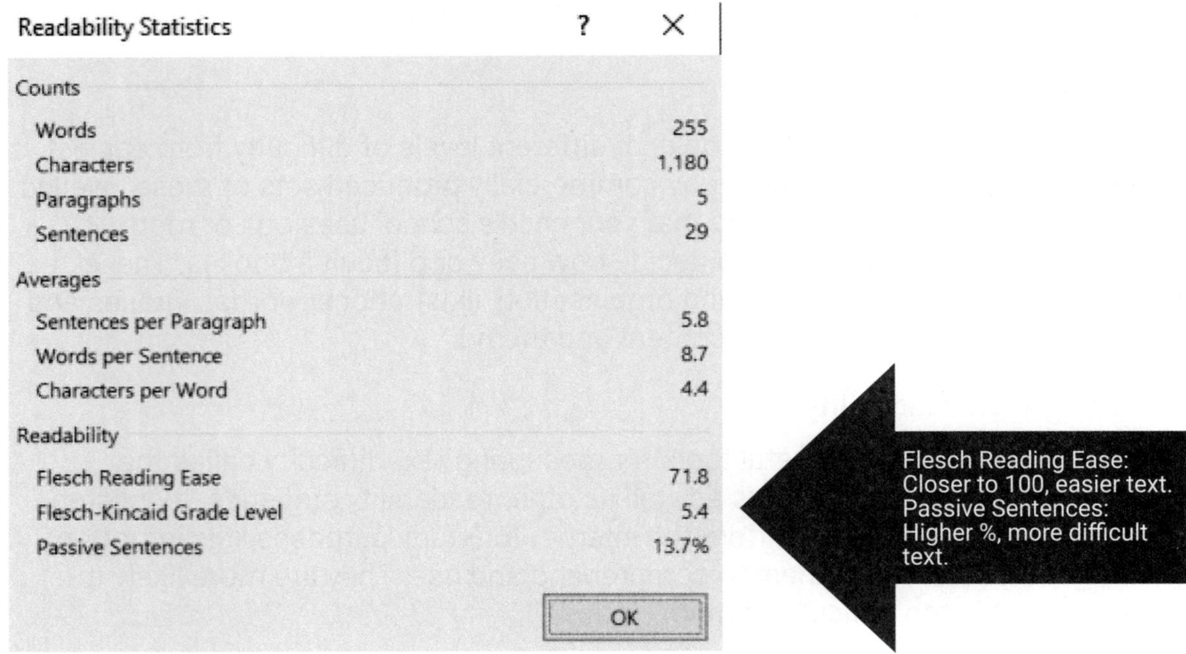

Flesch Reading Ease

This test rates text on a 100-point scale. The higher the score, the easier it is to understand the material.

Flesch–Kincaid Grade Level

This test refers to a grade or year level **not** age. Even though it is based on US year levels, the difference between those and Australian year levels is not significant.

Passive Sentences

The higher the percentage, the more difficult the text.

Texts on the same topic at different levels of difficulty

There are several internet sites where texts on the same topic at different levels of difficulty are available. At the time of publication of this book, these are some of them:

- https://newsela.com
- https://www.commonlit.org
- https://www.readworks.org (text to speech)

Appendix D: The 200 most common words in English

Many lists of the 200 most common (high frequency) words in English have been developed over time. Although there are slight differences between them, they are similar, so it does not really matter which one you use.

First 100 most common words in English

and	only	first	see	were
to	our	from	she	what
like	should	her	so	where
for	there	him	some	which
I	you	how	than	who
is	follow	if	the	will
other	about	in	their	wind
right	after	it	them	with
that	are	know	then	your
would	as	many	these	ask
time	at	may	they	year
look	be	my	thing	call
any	been	new	this	use
had	before	now	those	a
has	but	of	three	too
have	by	on	up	boy
he	can	or	very	man
made	could	out	was	off
more	day	over	way	all
one	do	said	we	get

Appendix D

Second 100 most common words in English

back	people	few	want	last
did	play	here	water	let
down	take	his	well	men
every	us	home	why	mother
find	went	into	come	name
found	when	keep	air	never
good	while	land	between	next
great	work	live	city	night
hand	give	must	does	no
help	again	not	don't	often
it's	also	old	eat	once
just	always	own	enough	part
left	an	put	even	place
little	another	say	friend	same
long	bother	small	go	saw
make	came	such	got	set
me	children	tell	head	show
most	each	think	hear	side
much	far	two	high	start
open	father	under	house	still

Appendix E: Prompts to help children develop inferential skills

Focusing on text-to-self connections:

- *What does this story remind you of?*
- *Can you relate to the characters in the story?*
- *Does anything in this story remind you of anything in your own life?*

Focusing on text-to-text connections:

- *What does this remind you of in another book you have read?*
- *How is this text similar to other things you have read?*
- *How is this text different from other things you have read?*

Focusing on text-to-world connections:

- *What does this remind you of in the real world?*
- *How are events in this story similar to things that happen in the real world?*
- *How are events in this story different from things that happen in the real world?*

Other question prompts to develop inference

Can you find an example of … ?

Can you think of another point of view about … ?

Can you think of another ending? Why?

How did … react to … ?

How does … feel about/after … ?

How does … relate to … ?

How is … different from … ?

How was … affected by … ?

How might you summarise the story?

If … had happened, what might the ending have been?

If you were … what would you have done? Why?

What did … most likely mean when they said … ?

What do … and … have in common?

What do you think the author means by … ?

What does the phrase/line … mean?

Appendix E

What is ...'s point of view about ... ?

What is the author implying when they write ... ?

What is the main idea of this paragraph?

What is the most likely reason for ... ?

What lesson can we learn from the story?

What reason/s does ... give for ... ?

What was the cause of ... ?

What were some of the motives behind ... ?

What would happen if ... ?

Where is the turning point in the story?

Which word best describes ...'s feeling about ... ? (Give some words, explain their meanings and ask the reader to choose one.)

Why did the main character say ... ?

Why do you think the author tells us ... ?

Why does the author include the character of ... ?

Why was the book set in ... ?

Bibliography

Annandale K, Bindon R, Handley K, Johnston A, Lockett L & Lynch P (2004a). *STEPS professional development: First Steps, reading resource book,* 2nd edn, Rigby Heinemann, Port Melbourne, Victoria.

Annandale K, Bindon R, Handley K, Johnston A, Lockett L & Lynch P (2004b). *STEPS professional development: First Steps, reading map of development*, 2nd edn, Rigby Heinemann, Port Melbourne, Victoria.

Archer AL & Hughes CA (2011). *Explicit instruction: effective and efficient teaching*, Guilford Press, New York.

Australian Association for the Teaching of English & Australian Literacy Educators' Association (2021). *MyRead*, Australian Literacy Educators' Association, Crows Nest, New South Wales, accessed 16 Apr 2021, https://www.alea.edu.au/publicresources/resources-for-teachers-and-educators/myread.

Beck IL, McKeown MG & Kucan L (2008). *Creating robust vocabulary*, Guilford Press, New York.

Beers K (2003). *When kids can't read, what teachers can do*, Heinemann Press, Portsmouth, New Hampshire.

Clay MM (1991). *Becoming literate: the construction of inner control*, Heinemann Education, Auckland, New Zealand.

Fisher D & Frey N (2008). *Word wise and context rich: five essential steps to teaching academic vocabulary*, Heinemann Press, Portsmouth, New Hampshire.

Fisher D, Frey N & Hattie J (2016). *Visible learning for literacy*, Corwin, London.

Fountas I & Pinnell GS (1991). *Guided reading: good first teaching for all children*, Heinemann Educational, Portsmouth, New Hampshire.

Fountas I & Pinnell GS (1999). *Matching books to readers: a book list for guided reading, K3*, Heinemann Educational, Portsmouth, New Hampshire.

High Frequency Words (nd). *Next 200 high frequency word lists*, High Frequency Words, accessed 16 Apr 2021, https://www.highfrequencywords.org/next-200-high-frequency-word-lists.html.

Macmillan B (1997). *Why schoolchildren can't read*, The Institute of Economic Affairs, Westminster, London.

Moats LC (2005). How spelling supports reading. *American Educator* Winter:12–43.

Bibliography

MultiLit Pty Ltd (2021). *Five from five*, MultiLit Pty Ltd, Macquarie Park, New South Wales, accessed 16 Apr 2021, https://fivefromfive.com.au.

Pinnell GS (2021). *What is leveled reading?* Scholastic, USA, accessed 16 Apr 2021, https://www.scholastic.com/teachers/articles/teaching-content/what-leveled-reading/.

Willis J (2008). *Teaching the brain to read: strategies for improving fluency, vocabulary and comprehension*, Hawker Brownlow, Moorabbin, Victoria.